reading aids series

Thinking Thursdays

language arts in the reading lab

Donna McKee Cleary
Mahwah, New Jersey, Public Schools

an ira *service bulletin*

international reading association • Newark, Delaware

Library of Congress Cataloging in Publication Data

Cleary, Donna McKee, 1948–
Thinking Thursdays.

(Reading aids series) (An IRA service bulletin)
Bibliography: p.
1. Developmental reading. 2. Reading–Remedial teaching. 3. Language arts–Remedial–teaching.
I. Title.
LB1050.53.C57 428′.4′3 78-4572
ISBN 0-87207-223-1

CONTENTS

FOREWORD

Most of the booklets published by the International Reading Association for the purpose of sharing information about reading or its pedagogy have their inception in one of the organized agencies of the Association—a committee, the Board of Directors, the Headquarters staff, etc. Only rarely does the Publications Division at Newark, Delaware, come into possession of an unsolicited single-author manuscript of such merit that it eventually becomes an official IRA publication. *Thinking Thursdays* is an exception; of the many manuscripts volunteered to the Director of Publications in recent months, this one was outstanding enough to be approved by the Publications Committee.

One of the most frequent questions directed to IRA staff members and officers (either by mail or at meetings of various sorts) is, "Where can I find some information about setting up a learning center (or a language experience program or a junior high school reading lab)?" While the Association's publication list includes many items which provide answers to such questions, none of the others gives such a personal account of the experiences of one professional educator who has recently faced the challenges and achieved the satisfactions of starting a program "from scratch." Donna McKee Cleary has written *Thinking Thursdays* with so much detail and such extensive description of her feelings that, in places, the content at times seems to be based on her diary. In any case, this booklet is unquestionably a "reading aid" for anyone establishing a secondary school reading laboratory.

Incidentally, the title, *Thinking Thursdays*, was rather cleverly derived. Read on, and find out how Author Cleary chose that name for her book.

William Eller, *President*
International Reading Association
1977-1978

IN THE BEGINNING

Two days before the opening of school, after a morning orientation session for new teachers, I first entered my classroom. Actually, it was my half-classroom, as a regular room had been divided by a temporary partition. The partition had only one shortcoming: it ended about three feet from the ceiling. Only once, however, after much muffled giggling from my students, did I observe the grinning jack-o-lantern face of an athletic sophomore bobbing between partition and ceiling.

A Goodly Stock of Materials, a Room

I had been assigned the inner half of this classroom, windowless and airless, but even that was an improvement over the book closet I had inhabited in an elementary school during my field experience as a reading teacher. The thought of having my own room—regardless of its dimensions and air quality—compensated for any inconveniences. I am by nature extremely territorial. I could not imagine myself a member of that nomadic breed of teachers known as "travelers," toting armloads of books and papers, racing the bell.

I had my own room! I tore the ragged vinyl curtains from the door's upper and lower windows, scraped from the pane a sticker that read "Zoo—Please Don't Feed the Animals" (it had been a remedial math room last year), and affixed fantastically-colored, four-inch-wide construction paper stripes to the windows. I dubbed it the Reading Resource Room, because it was a room (sort of), I was the resource (hopefully), and the students would be reading (what else?).

In the room were five carrels and fifteen student desks and chairs. There were no bookcases, no file cabinets, and no teacher desk. The tardy bookcases (four had been ordered months ago) were my primary concern. In an adjacent corridor was a budgetary phenomenon not to be believed: wall-to-wall cartons, stacked nearly waist-high, each carton labeled "Reading Department" but otherwise defying identification of contents. My English teacher friends were known for such peculiar behaviors as scavenging for paperbacks at garage sales and flea markets, and perusing stockroom shelves for a single novel written within the past decade. And I rejoiced heartily as I stood, amazed and overwhelmed, in the narrow aisle of Carton City.

Six broken fingernails and five hours later, I felt I had accomplished the impossible. (I had much to learn throughout the year about the meaning of "impossible.") I had eagerly explored every carton, checking contents against requisition forms. The empty boxes were piled in the hallway and, disheveled and perspiring in the early September heat, I sat in a state of sublime biblioecstasy amidst an incredible array of workbooks, filmstrips, textbooks, tachistoscopes, and reading kits.

Here was the "stuff." Here was the teacher. I would have six classes per day, fifteen students per class. Stuff and teacher had met. I was sure we would be happy together. But what about the students? Would they become the core of the curriulum? Would they respond to this avalanche of instructional materials?

In such an apparent haven of self-correcting, prelesson planned products, I might have heaved a sigh of relief at the prospect of a year in which I would have no units to devise, no tests to grade, no paperwork to do at home. I knew, in fact, that for these very reasons many content teachers have taken the extra graduate courses to become certified as teachers of reading. Of course, the decreased take home work and low student load didn't exactly cause revulsion in me. But I was eager to expand the focus of my previous teaching experience, during which I had involved myself and my students in a highly interactive teaching-learning relationship. I was also impelled to go beyond the use of impersonal materials, as the generative dynamism of a summer workshop at New York University was vibrating within me.

During the summer, I (and several other Master's candidates) had become intensely involved and personally committed to designing learning and teaching strategies in which the student was central. It was then that my needs and concerns were explored, and my potential as a human being and as a teacher were extended and expanded by Harold Vine, Marilyn Sobelman, and John Mayher of New York University's Graduate School of Education—three educators who practiced the student-centered teaching/learning that they advocated.

I truly hoped that, as a teacher, I would respond to the challenge of providing integrated learning experiences to meet the needs, concerns, and potentials of my own students. And thus I pondered, at last in my classroom, sitting among the workbooks, filmstrips, textbooks, and reading kits. If the students were to be the core of my reading program, how did I—boxed in at Carton City, without a kid in sight—plan to organize that program? And how did I know, assuming effective organization, that the program would work?

I glanced around the room, tilting my head this way and that, reading titles: *How to Study*; *Vocabulary for the High School Student*; *Vocabulary for the College Bound*; *Tactics in Reading*; *Reading for Understanding*; *Be a Better Reader*; *Better Reading*; *Reading for Young Adults*; *You Can Read Better*; *Reading for Meaning*. Do you get the idea? There were these titles and more, seemingly something for everyone. And each title sounded so definitive, so practical, so optimistic.

My Developmental Reading course was an elective open to students, grades 9–12, who scored one or two years below grade level on the California Test of Basic Skills, administered throughout the district. Being an elective, it was bound to attract motivated students. Because it was *developmental* reading, I would concentrate on developmental skills—i.e., improvement of slightly below average reading comprehension, rate, and vocabulary.

FLESH AND BLOOD ON THE STUDENT PROFILE

As I headed toward the parking lot late that afternoon, the Director of Guidance stopped me for a brief chat. He welcomed me to the school and asked if I had been apprised of the previous year's initial reading program. The first high school level reading specialist had begun by recruiting students from study hall and had devised a workable plan of such accomplishment and acceptance that a second teacher (myself) was required. I could see that this woman had already earned my gratitude. Her good work had created a job for me!

What I later discovered was that the Reading Specialist worked with groups of 6 for six periods per day. Her students scored more than two years below grade level on a standardized test. The Director of Guidance was getting to this point: there are more than 36 students in this category and they have been scheduled into Developmental Reading. He wanted to know whether that was workable. I cheerfully replied that my developmental students would be able to work with the remedial students to reinforce their own skills. The classes would be individualized. There was, after all, something for everyone.

The Elective that Wasn't

What I later discovered from the Reading Specialist and from the results of the standardized reading test we administered during the first week of school was that, among our combined student load of 126 pupils, only 3 could be described as developmental. The others were all technically remedial readers. Of those 123 pupils, the 36 with the most aberrant social, emotional, and academic records were assigned to Basic Reading with the specialist. The others, ranging from somewhat motivated to incredibly passive, were assigned in larger groups to Developmental Reading with the new reading teacher.

This new insight into the composition of my classes cast many shadows on my preconceptions about the "elective" nature of the course. "Strongly suggested," "insisted upon" were, without doubt, more accurate descriptions, for test scores and academic grades indicated that certain kids "needed" reading. It was assumed that I could diagnose their reading problems, prescribe individualized remedial or corrective medicine, and, hopefully, within a year, they would be well again. Once well, they would no longer need reading.

I soon discovered, however, that what my students needed could not be administered in medical dosages. They needed love, warmth, and success. They needed structure, accomplishment, and dignity. I felt I had been preparing all my life to teach these kids. I felt they needed *me*. But just what they needed from me I would not be able to name until we had struggled through a preoccupation with living up to the course title and shifted our emphasis to what reading and learning is really all about: THINKING.

THE SET-UP

The day before the first day of school I eagerly returned to my room. It was my last chance to prepare for the arrival of students. There was so much to be done! In addition to being extremely territorial, I also have this compulsion about being organized (a prerequisite, it turns out, for dealing with a dynamic reading program and the expectations of parents and administrators). My true spirit is probably chaotic and desultory, and I'm unconsciously compensating for that tendency; but, the fact remains, I *had* to have everything organized before the first day of school.

Ready, Set, Go

Along one of the walls of my room, I stacked the empty cartons in the semblance of a rather precarious, but functional, bookcase and loaded the cardboard shelves with the most immediately-identifiable-as-usable materials, an ostensibly positive panacea for curing the reading ills of my students.

From a cooperative manager at a local department store, I had acquired an antiquated display rack on which I arranged 200 paperback books. I brought in two wicker chairs from my grandmother's summer cottage, complete with thick, comfortable cushions. I also dragged in a 9 x 12 foot green shag rug—it wasn't new, but it served to delineate an informal reading corner.

I arranged the student desks in clusters of four and brought in from the hall a long table that seemed to be unclaimed. I covered the walls with the brightest, most philosophically positive posters I could find and stapled a collection of contemporary, thematically appropriate paperbacks to the wall under the staggered letters, INTERNAL CONFLICTS: YOU'RE NOT ALONE.

A seemingly benevolent math teacher offered me his old, wooden desk, sans drawer knobs, and I appreciatively accepted it. (I later discovered he had known about an imminent delivery of shiny, new, aluminum desks, with knobs and locks.) The desk did have quite a bit of character, though. I pushed it right up against the last empty wall, planning to sit at it only when I was alone in the room. With students working at individualized assignments, I knew I wouldn't spend much time at the desk during class. Also, the room was really too small for 15 students, a teacher, and a desk that was used simply to indicate who was who.

I set out my matching blotter, pencil holder, and notepad. My pencils were all imprinted with my name. (I thought this would discourage "borrowing;" instead, it made them collector's items.) I tacked up the class schedules and hung a calendar on which each day's "historical event" played with language, as *1821. Beekeeper Herman Kolp gets bad case of the hives.*

Between the ends of a wire bookrack on my desk, I lined up my professional texts and reference books. Setting my class lists in a neat pile on the blotter, I stepped back and looked around the room. It looked neatly organized, colorful, and alive. It looked like me—expectant, waiting—yet it needed something else: the kids. I didn't know exactly what might happen in this room, but I did know I liked it.

THE READING LAB

To establish structure and familiarize myself with the many and varied materials at my disposal, I organized a Reading Laboratory similar to those now available in most schools and colleges. The materials themselves greatly structure the program, as they are sequential, self-correcting, and valid *when matched to a student's weaknesses and strengths.* The teacher's manuals are likewise to be cherished as they explain all the how-to's, the purposes, and the results of the programs.

In an attempt to match the weaknesses and strengths of my students with the proper materials, I accepted the process of individually prescribed instruction, involving the assignment of specific remediation in areas of weakness as determined by standardized testing and continuous informal diagnosis.

Testing for Weaknesses

The Gates-MacGinitie Reading Test, Levels E and F, was administered to all students enrolled in reading classes. (Other group or individual tests are available.) The test is divided into three sections: Speed and Accuracy (short sentence or paragraph completions), Vocabulary (selection of a synonym for a word), and Comprehension (paragraph completion of increasing difficulty by selection of pairs of missing words). The test yielded national percentiles for all students and grade equivalents for ninth graders.

The majority of my students scored between the 20th and 34th percentiles, although some didn't even make the chart at all, scoring below the 2nd percentile. My interpretation of these scores to the students was that, of every 100 students your age and grade who take this test, you score better than 34 (or 21, or 8) of them. The above disclosure does not make for a thrilling student-teacher conference, and I was careful to be as gentle as possible with fragile egos. Yet I have never considered being less than frank about such facts. These kids have developed school behaviors that are as antagonistic as can be expected for the "bottom of the barrel." Being honest with them enables me to get across one point: I am not here to torture you with some arbitrary, punitive learning (work); I am here to help you remedy a real, measurable need. By shifting the responsibility for recognizing, accepting, and dealing with their deficiencies directly to the students, I establish a learning environment in which I am indeed a "resource" person, helping students do what they must for their own good. Believe me, they would love to see the daylight from the top of that barrel!

Establishing a System

After some experimentation with lab procedures (small group work turned into a three-ring circus), I arrived at the system described below. The students responded amazingly well to it and, by the end of October, the program was self-operative, the students were self-disciplined, and I was wrangling with an ambiguous skepticism. Were the kids learning from these programed materials all that the publishers had documented they would learn? Would the students' absolute belief in the efficacy of my "prescriptions" be justified?

Such questions could, of course, never be totally resolved due to the variables present within each student and within the reading process itself. Recognition of that fact helped me toward a healthy realism that alleviated the recurrent pangs of self-doubt and the compulsion to eradicate the deficiencies that had taken fifteen to seventeen years to congeal. I was no super teacher, as I had expected to be. With ninety students I couldn't even be sure which ones were simply marking random answers on their worksheets, or which ones were copying answers directly from the answer booklets. I tried to participate in the checking of answers as frequently as possible, and later learned strategies for making the students more accountable for their responses, but I'm sure a few quiet, inconspicuous students managed to beat the system. (Since they had managed to get to high school with such poor reading skills, they knew how to beat the system.)

Contracting for Performance

The system I established in the reading lab was a simple contractual agreement between the student and me. Three general areas for improvement were outlined: vocabulary (of primary importance because growth in this area might automatically improve the other two areas), comprehension, and rate. Improvement in rate does not imply the rapid reading techniques so well-advertised these days, but refers to the speed necessary to eliminate word-by-word reading to aid in the retention of the meaning of the beginning of a sentence by the time one gets to the end of the sentence.

Each teacher must select the materials he feels are most appropriate to the needs of the students, for purposes of motivation as well as content. I selected eight basic programs, from which my students and I could pick-and-choose appropriate lessons. One comprehensive kit that treats comprehension, vocabulary, and rate in each reading selection and corresponding exercises gives a unifying element to each student's program and also yields comparative scores for graphing individual progress.

Weekly Assignments

I devised several individual worksheets, finally refining them to the ones included at the end of this chapter. On these individual worksheets I recorded weekly assignments and noted completion of assignments. After a week's full-class orientation to each of the materials and the various machinery, students were given their worksheets daily as they entered the Reading Lab. Their weekly assignments had been indicated by yellow highlighter marks in the appropriate columns; as they completed the assignments, they recorded their scores over the yellow marks. If all indicated assignments were completed, the student had earned a *B* for the week. Extra assignments of his choice earned him an *A*, fewer assignments a *C* or a *D*. As everyone made an attempt to complete weekly assignments, there were no failures.

Each student's papers and answer booklets were kept in his own manila folder. The folders were identified by student name, grade, and class section. They were kept in a file cabinet (yes, it finally arrived) and were accessible to the student anytime during the school day.

Within the scope of the materials used, the assignments were individualized. Multileveled programs allowed me to diagnose entry level assignments for each student so, although they may have been using the same series or kit, fifteen students could easily be working on fifteen different levels. Each Friday, as I recorded a weekly grade (a requisite for the granting of credit toward graduation for reading instruction), I offered the student several options from which to select what I considered to be three sessions' worth of work for him. (What we did the other two days, in addition to the personal contract conferences, is yet to come.) Thereby, the student's contract for the following week was established.

The Lab Becomes Self-Operative

And so the reading lab functioned, seeming to meet student needs of immediate objectives and reinforcement and structure. The students entered the room, conformed to the atmosphere of efficient productivity, took their assignment sheets and folders, selected the necessary materials, worked independently throughout the period, recorded their scores on graphs and assignment sheets, returned their assignment sheets to me and their folders to the file cabinet, and exited.

For kids who had been back-rowers since elementary school—the passive minority, paying little attention to what the teacher in the front of the room was saying and understanding less (especially were it related to the reading assignments they could not, or would not, do)—the structured routine of a reading lab, in which each student is responsible and accountable on a daily basis for his own work (and that work is at the student's reading level) brought out the best work habits and behavior many of them had ever exhibited.

Yes, the reading lab had become self-operative, the students were incredibly self-disciplined (established standards of behavior were maintained even with a substitute teacher!), and I was still wrangling with my ambiguous skepticism.

Mahwah High School Developmental Reading Program/Student Worksheet

Name ______________ Grade ________ Semester ________ Year ________

Gates-MacGinitie Percentile Scores: A) Vocab. ___ Compreh. ___ Sp. ___ Acc. ___
B) Vocab. ___ Compreh. ___ Sp. ___ Acc. ___

IMPROVING SPEED, COMPREHENSION, and VOCABULARY:
CONTROLLED READERS

Level	Story #	Comp. %	Rate (w.p.m.)	Level	Story #	Comp. %	Rate (w.p.m.)

IMPROVING COMPREHENSION and VOCABULARY:
READING FOR UNDERSTANDING KIT

Practice	●	◆	■	▲	Comp. %	Practice	●	◆	■	▲	Comp. %	Practice	●	◆	■	▲	Comp. %
1						9						17					
2						10						18					
3						11						19					
4						12						20					
5						13						21					
6						14						22					
7						15						23					
8						16						24					

Mahwah High School Developmental Reading Program/Student Worksheet

IMPROVING COMPREHENSION and VOCABULARY:
READING LAB IVa

Color	Story #	Comp. %	Voc. %	Color	Story #	Comp. %	Voc. %	

IMPROVING VOCABULARY and COMPREHENSION:
WORD CLUES

Level	Lesson #	Flash-X Review	Level	Lesson #	Flash-X Review	

IMPROVING STUDY SKILLS, COMPREHENSION, and VOCABULARY:
SOC. STUDIES/REF. KITS

Level and #	Comp. %	Skill Description	Level and #	Comp. %	Skill Description

Mahwah High School Developmental Reading Program/Student Worksheet

SKILL DESCRIPTION *BE A BETTER READER SERIES*	Book I	Book II	Book III	Book IV	Book V
SYLLABICATION	p. 49__ p. 64__	p. 46__ p. 64__	p. 82__	p. 54__ p. 55__	X X
DISCOVERING PREFIXES and SUFFIXES	p. 138__ p. 139__	p. 76__ p. 118__	p. 48__ p. 98__	X X	X X
PREVIEW PROCEDURE	p. 12__ p. 13__ p. 14__	X X X	X X X	p. 16__ p. 17__ p. 18__ p. 19__	X X X X
HOW TO READ FAST	p. 36__ p. 52__ p. 69__	p. 16__ p. 17__	p. 115__ p. 130__	p. 8__ p. 9__ p. 10__ p. 11__ p. 12__ p. 13__ p. 14__	p. 9__ p. 10__ p. 11__ p. 12__ p. 43__ p. 46__
FINDING THE MAIN IDEA	p. 50__ p. 51__ p. 52__	p. 12__ p. 32__	p. 10__ p. 35__ p. 36__ p. 70__	p. 22__ p. 23__ p. 24__ p. 25__ p. 26__ p. 27__ p. 28__	p. 17__ p. 18__ p. 19__ p. 20__ p. 21__ p. 22__ p. 23__
DRAWING CONCLUSIONS	p. 122__	X	p. 72__ p. 127__	X	X
FINDING and ORGANIZING DETAILS	p. 67__ p. 68__	p. 49__ p. 60__ p. 61__	p. 86__	p. 29__ p. 30__	p. 26__ p. 27__ p. 28__ p. 29__ p. 30__ p. 31__ p. 32__
OUTLINING	p. 80__	p. 62__ p. 50__	p. 14__	X	p. 38__ p. 41__
TAKING NOTES	p. 125__	p. 134__	X	X	X
RESEARCHING	p. 120__ p. 121__	p. 123__ p. 124__	p. 128__ p. 129__	p. 129__ p. 130__	X
MAKING COMPARISONS	X	p. 106__	X	p. 116__ p. 117__ p. 118__ p. 119__	X

Mahwah High School Developmental Reading Program/Student Worksheet

SKILL DESCRIPTION *BE A BETTER READER SERIES*	Book I	Book II	Book III	Book IV	Book V
FINDING CAUSE and EFFECT	X	p. 91_	p. 52_	p. 125_ p. 126_ p. 127_ p. 128_	p. 51_ p. 52_ p. 53_ p. 54_ p. 55_ p. 56_ p. 115_
MAKING INFERENCES	X	X	p. 102_ p. 140_	p. 82_ p. 83_ p. 120_	p. 108_ p. 126_ p. 127_ p. 128_

READING BETWEEN THE LINES

The students learned to schedule their work, use their own judgment in selecting materials, and work independently and quietly. They consistently met their responsibilities in terms of classroom procedure and minimum work requirements. They behaved with dignity and respect toward me, toward themselves, and toward their classmates. Apparently, there are many peripheral learnings inherent in the individualized, programed instructional framework.

I knew it was a good program; I expected improved scores on my standardized posttest in May. But week-by-week, were my students making the same kinds of errors? Were they satisfied with a 70 percent score to the extent that they didn't bother analyzing the three wrong responses? I must admit that as I organized the reading lab—even as I thrilled to the effects of classroom management on disruptive, reluctant students—I harbored the belief that all those wonderful and beautiful materials could only test what a student already knew and really couldn't teach him what he didn't know (except, gradually, those crucial test-taking skills). There had to be truly individualized instruction—between individuals, between student and teacher—for new learning to occur. But with ninety students per day, how could I get to everyone?

An example of the limitations of programed instruction was disturbingly obvious—as demonstrated when four of my students used the *Reading for Understanding Kit*. Each girl professed to love working with the kit. Each was given a card slightly above her own working level. Each answered five RFU items.

This demonstration was given to graduate students in Harold Vine's Explorations in Reading: Experience and Process course at New York University. When all four girls indicated a correct response for one of the items, Vine probed for the reasoning underlying their selections. Not one girl based her rationale on the information in the RFU item! Their misinterpretation of the short reading selection was so gross that one girl supported her response by citing the exact opposite of the literal meaning of the item. Yet, each girl had chosen the "right" answer. Each girl then expressed the conviction that she had "learned" from doing the exercise.

The implications of such a demonstration are many and certainly deserve further research. One conclusion that may be tentatively advanced is that, based on individually prescribed instruction, reading instruction does indeed teach test-taking strategies, such as the elimination of incorrect responses based on syntax or length. However, exploration into the *process* of reading—that information-getting, pleasure-feeling process which we attempt to teach students—is severely limited by the Reading Lab situation.

Setting Goals

The specific goals of remedial reading instruction generally include improvement of vocabulary, comprehension, rate, and the acquisition of basic study skills. Texts on the teaching of reading and district curriculum guides meticulously delineate skill "ladders." I suppose we are to understand that skill by skill, rung by rung, students can pull themselves up the ladder until they become successful readers. If they can't, there are plenty of teachers, tutors, and workbooks to prod their reluctant legs upward toward the next, sequential rung.

Ignited by my educational colleagues, I began interpreting these skill ladders and cognitive experiences, not necessarily confined to the reading process, and not necessarily vertical. (According to James Moffett in *A Student-Centered Language Arts Curriculum*, an illiterate aborigine can draw conclusions and detect main ideas.) With one exception (see the case report on Chris in the Appendix), the students in my reading classes could decode the written language, could pronounce orally the printed word.

Why, then, did these kids score so far below actual grade placement on standardized tests? Why had they never read a book? Why were their grades in content subjects and their emotional problems attributed to "reading" deficiencies? Why did they so intensely hate to read? It seemed to me that they hated to read because they had never mastered the thought processes necessary for extracting *meaning and significance* from the printed page. They performed poorly in academic areas because they listened in the same inadequate way that they read. And they hated reading because the teaching of reading had been boring, punitive, judgmental, and isolated, with instruction seemingly aimed at some students' learning patterns but not at theirs.

The danger of continuing this type of reading instruction at the secondary level was summarized by Donald Moyle, President of the United Kingdom Reading Association, in a lecture at Montclair State College in 1974. "It is possible," he said, "that we have created a generation of more statistically-respectable nonreaders."

Moyle's words convey a greater significance today, as our schools are increasingly being held accountable for student performance on standardized tests of basic skills. While standardization of educational expectations is certainly respectable, the nature of reading must continue to transcend statistical standards.

Defining Thinking Skills

If students read unrelated selections (randomly of interest to them), answer the inevitable comprehension and vocabulary questions which trail along behind, and rarely discuss (if by any slim chance they thought it was worth discussing) what they have read with teacher or classmates, where in this pattern are we creating the joy of reading and the sense of purpose which will develop lifetime, independent readers?

I accept Moffett's theory that those skills commonly categorized as reading skills are actually thinking skills which, if they are developed, will be applied to the printed page as well as to any other mode of communication and behavior. It is a theory that is echoed and refined in the writings of the proponents of psycholinguistic reading theories.

So what thinking skills did my remedial students seem to need to develop? They needed to detect main ideas and supporting details; to make comparisons and contrasts; to organize information; to determine cause and effect relationships; to understand terms and concepts; to analyze tone and intent; to sequence ideas and events; to discover relationships among facts, generalizations, and values; to solve problems that require identification of the issue, consideration of causes of the issue, and evaluation of alternative solutions; to make judgments according to designated standards.

The secondary school reading teacher has one advantage which the elementary school teacher lacks. High school students have accumulated a broader experiential and oral language background. Perhaps the thinking skills have not been refined commensurate with experience or oral vocabulary. It becomes the teacher's responsibility, at every grade level, to be keenly aware of the thinking processes so crucial to effective reading and to provide for development of these thinking processes in every assignment and activity. (From this perspective, my students can again be called developmental.)

Thinking occurs internally. There is no way to evaluate students' thinking abilities unless they manifest them in some kind of external communication.

To allow students to manifest, explore, and develop their thinking abilities, the reading program must go beyond silent, individualized work.

Our reading specialist understood this well. The previous year, before reading was offered as a course for credit and grades, she had wisely interspersed programed instruction with informal discussions and games—word games, logic games, strategy games. When she suggested that we allow game playing in the reading rooms on Fridays, in addition to individual student-teacher progress conferences and contract setting, I immediately agreed. She felt intuitively that more learning occurred during a game of Anagrams or Scrabble (during which she could interact with her students in an informal situation and answer questions about spelling and word meanings), than usually took place within an isolated carrel between one student and the reading machine. It was a joy to see such excitement related to words.

Friday's routine was functional in that it was a necessary component of the individually prescribed instruction format, the contract-goal-setting, and it was fun in that oral communication was a natural outgrowth of the game playing and introduced a new element in individualization—personality.

What About Thursday?

Order had been established. Monday, Tuesday, and Wednesday were devoted to lab work. Friday was for conferences and games. And that left Thursday.

Thursday was my deliberate, contrived thinking skills day. I tried to elicit and challenge thinking skills every day in the classroom. I used a forum framework for verbalizing rationales for the selection of multiple-choice responses, with challenges to logic welcomed from the observers. I discussed responses with individuals whenever possible. But on *Thursdays* I could guarantee the emphasis for each student would be THINKING.

Thursday became known to the students as Group Day and, as the year progressed, by popular demand, Thursday sometimes lasted all week.

THURSDAY
or
WHAT'S FOR GROUP THERAPY TODAY?

The activities which follow are not sequential. However, within each activity are provisions for levels of participation and contribution to meet the needs of each student at his particular level of conceptual sophistication.

Because of this, these activities can be used with bright as well as remedial students, with elementary as well as secondary students, in reading classes as well as in the content areas. The accounts of each activity are intended only as models; the classroom teacher is certainly encouraged to adapt the activities to the students and the learning objectives with which he is working. Remember, if these activities worked with heterogeneous classes in which vocabulary level alone spanned eight to ten grades, they can certainly focus the attention of your students and, for your benefit as a teacher as well as for their growth, externalize their thinking skills.

Thinking for All

Preceding each account of Thursday's activities is a limited list of reading/thinking skills. I recommend writing these skills on the board for the sake of those students who have been conditioned to believe they can't be learning if they're having fun (and remedial students are prime proponents of this philosophy) and also for the sake of any faculty or administrative observers who may question the relevance of noise and activity in the "reading" room.

I have also attempted to express responses to Thursday's activities from the students' perspectives. Most of these thoughts are written in the students' words as they commented to me or their classmates. However, I couldn't entirely resist making assumptions about the feelings and reactions that were unspoken. Some of the student responses, therefore, include verbalizations of the silent language which communicates the unutterable between teacher and student.

GAYLE

I don't like nothin'
(especially talkin' in class)
So why did I say
"Bananas" when everyone was
staring at me?

Then she said to think crazy,
like Frank was maybe sitting
right in the classroom
with his skis on,
and Peter's head had been
replaced by a football.

And my yellow hair
was the color of bananas.

"That's Gayle, and she likes
bananas."
"That's Gayle, and she likes
bananas."

Everybody remembered my name.
Even the next day
Everybody remembered my name.

THURSDAY #1

On my first group-activity Thursday, I listed the following thinking/reading skills on the board:

attending to details
recalling details
associating previously unrelated facts

I used the Stanfords' "Getting Acquainted Activity," which involved seating the group in a circle. Each member of the group gave his name and a positive statement—something he *liked.* (Otherwise all would have said, "I hate reading.") Volunteers then tried to name each member in the circle and recall their identifying characteristic. When a volunteer was stumped, the *forgettable* person again supplied the information about himself, and the volunteer continued around the circle.

I tried to give every member of the group a chance to recite the information, allowing the more reluctant ones to go last, thereby hearing the information many times and benefiting from the mnemonic devices by which I was associating name to *like*.

When everyone had a turn, I asked the group to try to remember the names and *likes* of their classmates for the next day, when I would convene the circle for about five minutes of *memory* review.*

*Thursdays #2, 4, and 5 were adapted from *Learning Discussion Skills Through Games* by Gene Stanford and Barbara Dodds Stanford. New York: Citation Press, 1969, 19–30.

ROBERT

Get me a pencil.
How tall are you?
Well, dummy, stand up
next to Dave . . .
she *said* you could proximate.
You're 5′10″", okay?
Awright now,

5′10″
5′2″
5′8″
5′9″
———
5′29″

Okay, our average height is
7′5″
Y'know, could be somethin' wrong here . . .

THURSDAY #2

Skills:

- determining relevant data
- concentrating on a task
- organizing data
- planning procedure
- solving a problem

I divided the class into three groups of five. Each group was to determine the average height, in feet and inches, of their group. If a group member didn't know his height, he was told to approximate by comparing his height to that of another group member. The group had to agree on the method of determining the answer before submitting it to the teacher.

The groups took this as a competitive task and each tried to be the first to complete the task. During the same period, the groups were asked to determine their average weight. Since they had begun by racing the clock to complete the tasks, I made up a tie-breaker: For every blue eye, give your group 2 points; for every green eye, subtract 4 points; for every brown eye, add 1 point. The group with the highest *eye* quotient won, but all students had interacted using problem-solving strategies.

DONALD

Read it again,
read it again.
What was that about the
steam on the bathroom window?

Can we hear it one more time?

(I want to be the one to
figure it out!)

I think I've got it now.
Shh, don't let the other group
hear.

I know who did it.

THURSDAY #3

Skills:

attending to details
analyzing information
considering alternatives
judging incongruities
evaluating data
drawing conclusions

Again I divided the class into three groups. They were instructed to listen carefully to a short mystery story and decide what *incongruous* statement (every occasion an occasion for teaching vocabulary) revealed the guilty party to a seemingly *omniscient* detective.

In their groups they were to discuss the possibilities and persuade the others of their point-of-view by supporting statements with reasons based on the short mysteries.

This became a favorite Thursday activity, and I repeated it at intervals. Excellent sourcebooks for the detective tales are Donald J. Sobel's *Two-Minute Mysteries* and *More Two-Minute Mysteries* (New York: Scholastic Book Services, 1967 and 1971).

If a group offered an incorrect hypothesis, they were instructed to try again, recalling the specific details of the mystery. The group situation was excellent for stimulating individual contributions, as different students could recall different, and often essential, details.

MARK

I'd do better on my own.

Man, I told them they'd need
a stellar map, but

Brains here

didn't even know what it was,
just that we wouldn't need it.

He wanted the matches.

(Yeah, they'd be *real* helpful
on the moon.)

THURSDAY #4

Skills:

vocabulary development
problem solving
considering alternatives
evaluating opinions
substantiating one's own opinions
persuading
recalling pertinent data from past experiences
speculating about consequences of decisions
planning action
forming a consensus

This "Lost on the Moon" game, devised by Jay Hall of the University of Texas School of Business Administration, was based on actual work performed by the National Aeronautics and Space Administration. It is explained in *Learning Discussion Skills through Games* (*15*).

I distributed to each student the problem description (which appears on the following page). Without consultation with classmates, each student was to rank the items in order of importance. Then the students broke into five groups of three to arrive at a group consensus. Having already determined their personal list of priorities, students now had to compromise or convince. When the correct NASA ranking is distributed, students can decide whether they would fare better on their own resources or with the input of others.

For a little atmosphere, I tacked on the bulletin board two full color posters of the first moon walk.

LOST ON THE MOON

You are in a space crew originally scheduled to rendezvous with a mother ship on the lighted surface of the moon. Mechanical difficulties, however, have forced your ship to crashland at a spot 200 miles from the rendezvous point. The rough landing damaged much of the equipment aboard. Since survival depends on reaching the mother ship, the most critical items available must be chosen for the 200 mile trip. The fifteen items left intact after the landing are listed below. Your task is to rank them in terms of their importance to your crew in its attempt to reach the rendezvous point. Place number 1 by the most important item, number 2 by the second most important item, and so on through the least important item, number 15.

______ Box of matches
______ Food concentrates
______ 50 feet of nylon rope
______ Parachute silk
______ Portable heating unit
______ Two .45 caliber guns
______ One case dehydrated milk
______ Two 100-pound tanks of oxygen
______ Stellar map of the moon's constellations
______ Life raft containing CO_2 bottles
______ Magnetic compass
______ 5 gallons of water
______ Signal flares
______ First-aid kit containing injection needles
______ Solar-powered FM receiver-transmitter

ANSWER SHEET

Below are the correct rankings for the items, as determined by the space survival unit of NASA:

15 Box of matches (little or no use on the moon)
4 Food concentrate (supply daily food required)
6 50 feet of nylon rope (useful in tying injured, help in climbing)
8 Parachute silk (shelter against sun's rays)
13 Portable heating unit (useful only if party landed on dark side)
11 Two .45 caliber guns (self-propulsion devices could be made from them)
12 One case dehydrated milk (food, mixed with water for drinking)
1 Two 100-pound tanks of oxygen (fills respiration requirements)
3 Stellar map of the moon's constellations (one of principal means of finding directions)
9 Life raft (CO_2 bottles for self-propulsion across chasms, etc.)
14 Magnetic compass (probably no magnetized poles; thus, useless)
2 5 gallons of water (replenishes loss by sweating)
10 Signal flares (distress call whthin line of sight)
7 First-aid kit containing injection needles (oral pills or injection medicine valuable)
5 Solar-powered FM receiver-transmitter (distress signal transmitter, possible communication with mother ship)

CHRIS

Okay, now let's get this straight—

Who has clues with times in them?

Yeah. Yeah. Got it.
Anybody else?

Then why have you just been
sitting there?

Okay, now what about the days?

Wednesday? How do you spell that?

I know. I know. You're not so
brilliant yourself or you wouldn't

Be HERE.

Forget it. Somebody else write
on the board.

Oh. Okay. Who has clues with
places in them?

THURSDAY # 5

Skills:

- considering and evaluating information
- organizing information for problem solution
- noting supportive or contradictory details
- drawing conclusions
- making inferences
- evaluating data
- following time-place sequence
- character analysis
- vocabulary development

It seemed that the kids never got tired of solving mysteries. And I really can't think of any thought process or reading skill that wasn't somehow stimulated by solving mysteries. The following game was devised by the Stanfords to teach the discussion skills of organizing for problem solving and recognizing the value of all contributions.

The class sat in a circle on the rug in my reading corner. To each student I distributed one or two clues. Each clue was intended to help the *group* solve a murder mystery. If the students could organize all the facts, they would be able to solve the mystery.

I told them to find the *murderer*, the *weapon*, the *time* of the murder, the *place* of the murder, and the *motive*. When the group agreed on answers to those items, they could submit their conclusions to me. However, if any one fact was incorrect, I would reject their solution and wait for them to resubmit the correct one.

The only rules were that no one could move around the circle, nor could clues be passed around. Most groups began by reading aloud their clues. But a random reading of clues usually yielded little insight. As the group became increasingly organized, clues were read aloud in categories such as those relating to time, place, etc.

On subsequent Thursdays, I used both clue sets from the Stanfords' book. At the request of my students, I devised a third mystery clue set, which appears at the end of this chapter. To preserve all three sets of mystery clues, I typed each clue on a 3 x 5 inch card and covered it with clear contact paper.

Related to the mystery approach to reading/thinking skills, I also used the materials in an issue of Scholastic's *Scope*. Two dramatic recordings of mystery theaters were included in the teacher's edition. While the students listened to the recordings, they kept important facts and character identifications on a worksheet provided in their copies of *Scope*.

A popular addition to Game Day was Selchow and Righter's *Mystery and Detective Game* which, in addition to all the aforementioned variables, included alibis and descriptions of suspects and weapons dependent on adjective cards.

MYSTERY CLUE SET #3

Mr. and Mrs. Nathaniel Kent reside in a ranch home in Franklin Lakes, New Jersey.

The time of Claudia Preston's death was determined to be six days after she was scheduled to fly as a stewardess to Italy.

Blood was found on the steering wheel of the Kents' car.

Mrs. Kent visited her hospitalized mother on Wednesday and Thursday nights at Chilton Hospital.

Mr. Nathaniel Kent works in New York City.

Claudia Preston purchased cork sandals, a glass figurine, and an original oil painting in Italy.

The doorman at Mr. Kent's apartment building was able to identify a photograph of Claudia Preston.

Mrs. Kent met her husband at his office around eight o'clock Monday night. They went out to dinner, returning home about 1 a.m.

Claudia Preston is a stewardess for TWA.

Neighbors told police they heard violent arguments coming from Mr. Kent's apartment on Monday, Tuesday, Wednesday, and Thursday nights of the week of the murder.

Claudia Preston was scheduled to fly to Italy on the Saturday before her death and return to the United States the following Friday.

A ceramic figurine was found broken on the floor in Nathaniel's New York City apartment.

Claudia Preston is a twin.

Mrs. Kent played bridge with her friends on Tuesday night.

Neighbors told the apartment superintendent the same story about the violent arguments that they told the police.

Claudia Preston's body was found on the living room rug in Mr. Kent's apartment.

The superintendent of Mr. Kent's apartment building often received complaints about the loud stereo system Mr. Kent usually played until midnight during the week.

Claudia Preston's twin did the October centerfold for a famous women's liberation magazine.

Answer: The victim was Claudia Preston. It could be assumed that she and Mr. Kent had been arguing during the week prior to her murder; however, she had been to Italy as evidenced by her purchases. Among the purchases was the murder weapon, the *glass figurine*. It could be assumed that Mrs. Kent may have murdered her husband's mistress, but she had alibis for the entire week. It could be assumed that Claudia's twin was also having an affair with Kent and killed her sister, or that the sister was killed and the body misidentified. However the final clue indicates that Claudia's twin was a male, so the twin was just a distraction. The arguments had been taped by Mrs. Kent and an accomplice and played during the week. *Mrs. Kent* was the murderer, and the place was Kent's apartment. The motive was jealousy. The time was Friday.

LYNN

Glide?
Shore?
Snow?
Beach?

What the hell word can that be?

Seaside.
New Jersey.
Waves.
Sand.

I got it–*COAST*!

THURSDAY #6

Skills:

- attending to verbal clues
- relating clues to determine meaning
- vocabulary development through use of synonyms, antonyms, and word associations

Password, a popular television game show and home game, seemed to offer possibilities for vocabulary development. However, both versions are played by only four participants. To adapt this game to the classroom situation, I divided the class into two teams. Each team sits in a small circle.

From each team, one "contestant" is given the same "password." The contestants may then return to their seats in their team's circle. By alternately giving a clue to members of their own team, in clockwise order, the contestants attempt to help their own teammates guess the password.

For example, contestants #1 from groups A and B are given the password *adolescent*. The contestant from group A gives a one-word clue to the person immediately to his left. If the teammate's response (worth 10 points) is incorrect, the contestant from group B gives a one-word clue to the person in his group immediately to his left. If the password is guessed on the second clue, it is worth 9 points, and so on. Only one person may respond to a clue, team members waiting their turns in clockwise order.

The strategy, of course, is for each player to listen carefully to clues and responses given by each team, and try to determine a common line of thought or to distinguish between contradictory clues. Passwords can be randomly selected or culled from vocabulary lists.

DWIGHT, SHEILA, and ELLEN

Get a whiff of #7–
It is *nasty*–
Smells like the locker room.

"Gee, I hope I don't get
Detention. That room is so small–
and no windows–
I'd just *die*!"

What are those black things
you stick in ham?
How do you spell it?

"Boy, I'm sure glad this
school isn't on top of a hill!
I'd *never* be here!"

You mean I can't write down the
ten things *while* my hand is in
the bag? I have to remember them?

THURSDAY #7

Skills:

memory
vocabulary development
sensual awareness and sensual discrimination
role-playing
writing and spelling
making inferences

Students were prepared for Phobia Day by completing a worksheet (following) on which they defined and listed as many phobias as they could find in the dictionary. They were allowed to create original phobias using Latin roots, such as barbaphobia (fear of whiskers).

Students were then instructed to select a phobia of their choice and, during class on Thursday, to exhibit behavior and conversation that would be typical of a person having such a phobia. No direct statement of phobia was permitted. At the end of the period, the students attempted to identify the phobia which each person had exhibited during class.

To provide the students with an informal atmosphere in which to exhibit their phobias (it was Halloween week), the Resource Room was arranged in "sense" centers. There was a grab bag, an olfactory center (ten paper cups with smelly things wrapped in each), a visual center (perceptual puzzle posters), and a count-the-beans jar.

Students were provided with worksheets on which they could record the items felt in the grab bag, the ten smells, the number of beans, and the answers to the perceptual puzzles. At the bottom of the worksheet were a list of studied phobias and a space to record phobias their classmates had exhibited during the period (worksheets follow).

PHOBIA: fear, dislike, aversion

The root *phobia* is itself a complete word. Children may have "school phobia" or "ghost phobia" or "lion phobia." Their fear may be real or imagined. Likewise, adults may have a phobia of the dark, a phobia of responsibility, or a phobia of death.

Check the dictionary to determine whether phobias are rational or irrational. (Underline your choice.)

Is a phobia a mild dislike or extreme fear? (Underline your choice.)

Write a definition for *phobia*: ______________________________
____

____

Phobia is the root of each of these ten words. Use a dictionary to define them.

acrophobia ______________________________
agoraphobia ______________________________
Anglophobia ______________________________
claustrophibia ______________________________
Germanophobia ______________________________
hydrophobia ______________________________
monophobia ______________________________
phobia ______________________________
photophobia ______________________________
xenophobia ______________________________

Exercise: Complete each of the following sentences.

1. You wouldn't expect a mountain climber to have ____________.

2. As we grow up, we overcome our childhood ______________ of the dark.

3. His ________________ prevented him from swallowing liquids.

WHAT DOES YOUR NOSE KNOW?

1. ____________
2. ____________
3. ____________
4. ____________
5. ____________
6. ____________
7. ____________
8. ____________
9. ____________
10. ____________

HOW WELL DO YOU FEEL?

1. ____________
2. ____________
3. ____________
4. ____________
5. ____________
6. ____________
7. ____________
8. ____________
9. ____________
10. ____________

PUZZLING PUZZLES

1. ____________
2. ____________
3. ____________
4. ____________
5. ____________

HOW MANY PEAS? ____________

PHOBIA	WHO HAS IT?
1. acrophobia	____________
2. agoraphobia	____________
3. Anglophobia	____________
4. claustrophobia	____________
5. Germanophobia	____________
6. hydrophobia	____________
7. monophobia	____________
8. Russophobia	____________
9. necrophobia	____________
10. phobia of ____________	____________
11. phobia of ____________	____________
12. phobia of ____________	____________
13. phobia of ____________	____________
14. phobia of ____________	____________
15. phobia of ____________	____________

MARK

It's not hard to guess who
the can of Bud is.
Do you have a flip-top, too,
Coop?

Hey, Elisa, which one are you?
The frog? The balloon?
C'mon, which one?

(Bet you couldn't guess me.
Or maybe you could.
Maybe I wish you would.)

THURSDAY #8

Skills:

using symbolic language
writing, spelling, reading
making inferences
generalizing
evaluating

This activity was used by Harold Vine in a summer graduate course to contrast teacher-centered lessons with student-centered lessons. It was as effective with remedial high school students as with Vine's graduate students.

Each student was instructed to write a single sentence beginning with the words "I am . . . " and naming a favorite animal or inanimate object, followed by some description of an action. Two examples were given: "I am a fawn drinking at a cool brook." and "I am a soccer ball scoring the winning goal."

As the students completed their sentences, a class secretary wrote each statement on the board. The class automatically began to avidly read the statements, correct spelling errors, and speculate about who wrote what.

When all the statements were on the board, another sheet of paper was distributed to each student. Next to the statement numbers, the students indicated the name of the classmate believed to have authored each. Another student tabulated the data on the board and, as the results poured in, conclusions were drawn as to which attributes the class identified with individual members.

To protect individuals, judgments were never verified; but, in addition to intense writing and reading, every member of the class received some feedback about how his peers view him.

TERRY

How am I supposed to know
the right answers?

How am I supposed to do this
if I don't drive?

I know, I know, *assume*
I'm driving and
after all
I *have* been a passenger . . .
I heard you tell Joe.

Well . . .
when we get in groups
I want some seniors in mine.

THURSDAY #9

Skills:

selecting appropriate responses
relating problems to past experiences
considering alternatives
vocabulary development
drawing conclusions
evaluating conclusions

Everyone loves to take self-analysis quizzes. Many periodicals regularly feature such quizzes. This year I found two terrific quizzes in a magazine, one quiz was titled "Would You Survive?" and the other, "How Good a Driver Are You?"

To structure a classroom lesson using these magazine quizzes, I made a poster indicating interpretation of scores and copied the quizzes and the correct answers with the magazine's explanations. As in "The Moon Game," I asked students first to take the quizzes individually, then arrive at a consensus within small groups, and finally compare how well they fared alone versus participation in a group.

Discussion of personality analyses yielded by quiz scores was always lively, and I was thrilled when students could disagree with the rationale behind the magazine's determination of correct answers.

The scoring poster for the driving quiz read:

Give yourself one point for each correct answer.

22–24 points: You're a super driver—skillful, knowledgeable, and relaxed behind the wheel.

16–21 points: Average good driver—you're apt to be unsure of yourself in emergencies.

Less than 15: Hitchhike!

FRANK

What's the stopwatch for?
Oh, no.

I don't understand what
we're doing.

"Frank, would you shut up
and listen
so she can tell you?"

Am I in the picture?
Just looking out the front
window?

I don't see anything wrong
there.
Nothing.

Wait, wait!
Yeah, I see it now,
I see it!

THURSDAY #10

Skills:

perceptual discrimination
writing
comparing answers (paraphrases)
attending to details
vocabulary development

Using a free Shell Corporation filmstrip, "Perception of Driving Hazards" (write to SHELL FILM LIBRARY, 1443 Sadlier Cir. W. Dr., Indianapolis, Indiana 46239), I instructed my students to jot down the hazard(s) they observed during a 15-second exposure of numbered frames. Two sample scenes were provided to familiarize the class with the activity.

After a 15-second exposure, the picture frame was removed from the screen and the filmstrip advanced to a blank frame. At that time, each student recorded whatever hazards he perceived in the frame. After all twenty frames were exposed and students had recorded their perceptions, I distributed copies of the Shell Filmstrip Commentary.

I rewound the filmstrip and, as each frame was reviewed for longer periods of time, students compared their answers with the commentary sheet (see the following).

Filmstrip Commentary

Each scene is followed by an end frame with a letter or number identification of the scene. The filmstrip starts with two sample scenes, which the instructor or group leader should use to familiarize the group with the nature of the activity to be engaged in.

Sample A: Here we have a tree shadowed, curving road. It may be difficult to make out the situation that lies ahead. Obviously, caution and reduced speed are called for.

Sample B: There is a truck on your right and a car on your left. The hazard is rather subtle here. What is the clue to the hazard? (Answer: The car on your left has its front wheels turned slightly toward your lane of traffic. You face a possible "squeeze play.")

NOW THE FILMSTRIP PROPER BEGINS. AFTER EXPOSURE OF A SCENE, DISCUSSION DURING THE SUBSEQUENT "NUMBERED FRAME" PERIOD MAY WARRANT THE INSTRUCTOR'S TURNING BACK TO THE SCENE IN ORDER TO POINT OUT ITS DETAILS. DO NOT DISCOURAGE THE IDENTIFICATION OF POSSIBLE HAZARDS OTHER THAN THOSE MENTIONED IN THE COMMENTARY BELOW.

Scene 1. This is a tight situation for you (note the front of your car's hood). The car directly in front of your car is pulling out of your lane (no turn light is on) because immediately ahead a cab has stopped to pick up a passenger. What would you do under these circumstances?

Scene 2. A simple and very serious hazard. You are tailgating a truck. How does this affect you in terms of possible maneuvers?

Scene 3. Here we have a slow-moving, or perhaps stopped, street sweeper in your lane ahead. Notice, too, the vehicle in the lane to your left. What about your speed in this situation?

Scene 4. The water along the right side of the road is obvious, and normally to be avoided. But how about the car at the intersection, which is turning into your street? What is the desirable action for you to take?

Scene 5. This fairly busy, small town street would present no special problem for you if it were not for . . . . (Answer: a pedestrian apparently about to emerge from between parked cars on your side of the road.)

Scene 6. You're fairly close to a school bus . . . practically tailgating it. Tailgating is a major factor in accidents and the fact that you're fairly close to a *school bus* makes it even more serious.

Scene 7. One perceptual clue is particularly important here: the opening door of a car on your right a short distance ahead.

RICHARD

Let's try it without the
guide card.

You keep score.

Mrs. Wirtz'll go ca-razy
if we learn these nouns
for the quiz tomorrow.

"How come those two are
playing cards?"

These aren't just cards!

THURSDAY #11

Skills:

vocabulary development
associating related data

Ruminare (to think) was designed to meet the needs of several of my students who were understandably having difficulty mastering Latin vocabulary lists.

Ruminare is a rummy game in which a "set" consists of the Latin word (printed as it would appear in an English dictionary, indicating derivation); definition of the Latin word; and two English derivatives. In the deck I included a rules card and a guide card, listing all complete sets. Players were allowed to lay down three of a set and received extra points for playing all four cards of a set. Regular rummy rules applied. The deck consisted of 15 Latin root words; that is, 60 cards total.

Although several companies manufacture rummy decks, most of them are developed for elementary school children, stressing vowel sounds and rhymes. I discovered the incredible diversity of the rummy deck when my colleague, Mary, began creating deck after deck of Synonym Rummy and Category Rummy for her students.

The kids love to play cards and can soon form appropriate sets without the aid of a guide card. It proved a fantastic technique for introducing new vocabulary words (in a set of familiar synonyms). Mary is now working on decks to accompany the text used by our English Department. The cards are made from heavy oaktag cut into 3 x 4 inch rectangles.

[< L. *barba*] 4	beard 3
barber 2	barb 1

Sample "set" of *Ruminare* cards

BOB

C'mon, we have
time
for one more!

Let me make up
the sentence!

. . . or how about a
quickie:

__________ you
or
mother __________

No, really
there's a LOT of
words you could
fit in there:

mother *dear*
mother *goose*
mother *of pearl*
mother *mia*
(that's Italian!)

THURSDAY #12

Skills:

contextual analysis
spelling
reading
general comprehension

Once again a television quiz show inspired what I think is a great reading activity. On the TV version of the *Match Game*, the emcee reads a sentence or short paragraph in which a word has been omitted. Each of the six members of the celebrity panel writes a word that could complete the sentence. The contestant responds orally with the word he would use to complete the sentence. The celebrities show their answer cards, one by one. Each celebrity answer which matches the contestant's answer scores one point for the contestant.

In my classroom adaptation, I wrote a short sentence on the board or on a transparency leaving out a crucial word. For example, one item might read: "Leonard was so disgusted he dropped his books in the ________." Each member of the class had a turn to be the contestant. The contestant thinks of his fill-in, while the rest of the class members write their responses on 5 x 7 inch cards. When all writing is completed, the contestant gives his response orally and writes it in the blank (if the board is being used). One by one, the others show their answers (they recognize their own spelling errors). The contestant's score is the number of classmates who matched his answer. The winner is the student with the highest score.

To break ties, a single word is given, such as Snow ______ or Sleepy ______. Everyone *writes* his response, and the tie is broken when one of the tying contestants scores more matches than the other.

As with many of my Thursday activities, this spontaneously became student-directed, as kids offered to compose the sentences and write them on the board. Sample sentences, written by students, are listed below.

1. Whenever Alvin's mother yelled at him, he just wanted to ________.
2. Theodore wore his best ________ to the Prom.
3. After a boring day at school, all Jim could think of was ________.

4. Phoebe had four brothers, three sisters, and two __________.

5. Jerry turned his stereo up, closed the door, and started to __________.

6. For her birthday, Diane received a three-pound __________.

BILL

You mean like
free association?
Just write whatever
word
you think it is?
Any word?

Okay, so it's easier
in sentences–
And if we remembered
SQ3R
It's even easier.

Yep, I think I get it.

(So why did I spend
three years
and tears
learning what a
long vowel said?)

THURSDAY #13

Skills:

decoding
contextual analysis
comparing data
drawing conclusions (about the reading process and about the value of previewing)

This activity was an outgrowth of an exercise used by Harold Vine in his Explorations in Reading course. His initial experiment was to determine the frequency of error when consonant groups, listed vertically, were translated into words, as compared to frequency of error when consonant groups, appearing in sentences and familiar quotations, were translated into words. The conclusions drawn by his graduate students were that linguistic and syntactic clues aided the decoding process and that errors were further decreased when the reader was familiar with the context in which the consonant groups appeared.

Adapting this exercise to my remedial classes, I prepared a list of 40 consonant groups, extracted from a lesson on the SQ3R study method to which all students had been introduced earlier in the year. The list of 40 words was projected through an overhead transparency. The students were instructed to number their papers from 1 to 40, and write the word they believed each consonant group represented.

Appearing on a second transparency, also transcribed in the consonants-only code, were the eight steps of the SQ3R method. These sentences included all the consonant groups which had been listed on the first transparency. Those 40 consonant groups were underlined for scoring purposes.

On the reverse side of their papers, students were instructed to transcribe the eight coded sentences in correct English. Copies of both transparencies are included at the end of this section.

As volunteers read aloud the complete sentences, students marked those underlined words which were incorrect (similar to a cloze test). Then students compared their lists of 40 individual words against the "correct" list which I read to them. The number of nonmatching responses was tallied by each student.

A comparison of nonmatching responses on side 1 (the list) to nonmatching responses on side 2 (complete sentences) consistently yielded a higher number of nonmatching responses on the listed consonant groups.

As a student tabulated results of this experiment on the board, the following conclusions were drawn by my remedial reading students:

You can read better when words are in sentences.

You can read pretty good without vowels.

You can read faster by just looking at certain consonants.

You can read faster by looking at whole sentences.

If you already know something about what you're reading, you can read better.

My students responded extremely well to the experimental framework in which this exercise was presented. They told me they enjoyed participating in the experiment. Many remarked they had learned something about their own reading problems and about some of the disadvantages of reading word-by-word rather than in contextual word-groups.

The experiment also stimulated conversation about my students' early reading experiences. Apparently, as they tried to break this new consonants-only code, they reactivated personal feelings associated with their initial reading instruction.

Transparency #1

1. stdy ________	15. qstns ________	29. spd ________
2. th ________	16. nd ________	30. nds ________
3. ttl ________	17. thnk ________	31. cls ________
4. lk ________	18. abt ________	32. bk ________
5. sbhds ________	19. whch ________	33. rvw ________
6. pctrs ________	20. my ________	34. mn ________
7. thr ________	21. b ________	35. mprtnt ________
8. cptns ________	22. nswrd ________	36. dtls ________
9. chrts ________	23. n ________	37. rct ________
10. mps ________	24. yr ________	38. wrtg ________
11. rd ________	25. rdg ________	39. lssn ________
12. th ________	26. hdgs ________	40. syng ________
13. chptr ________	27. crflly ________	41. ald ________
14. smry ________	28. djst ________	42. tst ________

Transparency #2

1. *Stdy th ttl.*
2. *Lk* at *sbhds*; *pctrs* nd *thr cptns*; *chrts*, *mps*, nd thr cptns.
3. *Rd th chptr smry* (or 1st prgrph).
4. Rd the *qstns* at th *nd* of th chptr.

5. *Thk abt* qstns *whch my b nswrd n yr rdg*. Chng ttls, *hdgs*, nd sbhdgs nto qstns.
6. Rd *crflly*; *djst* yr *spd* to yr *nds*.
7. *Cls* yr *bk* nd *rvw*. Rcll the *mn* ids; rcll th *mprtnt dtls*.
8. *Rct* by *wrtg* nts abt th *lssn*, *syng* it *ald*, or tkng a *tst*.

Italicized words on transparency #2 correspond to numbers 1–42 on transparency #1. The eight steps of the SQ3R study method are:

1. Study the title.
2. Look at subheads; pictures and their captions; charts, maps, and their captions.
3. Read the chapter summary (or first paragraph).
4. Read the questions at the end of each chapter.
5. Think about questions which may be answered in your reading. Change titles, headings, and subheadings into questions.
6. Read carefully; adjust your speed to your needs.
7. Close your book and review. Recall the main ideas; recall the important details.
8. Recite by writing notes about the lesson, saying it aloud, or taking a test.

LARRY

The pair?
The part?
The parents?
The Parent Game?
A partridge in a pear tree?
The Partridge Family!

THURSDAY #14

Skills:

- rapid reading
- categorizing
- guessing at words from minimal grapheme clues

An ideal follow-up to the previous experiment was my adaptation of the television quiz, *Baffle*. On the TV version, two pairs of celebrities compete against the clock to get their partner to identify a phrase or title (within a specified category) by exposing three consonants, then adding an additional consonant every five seconds until the phrase or title is guessed.

To adapt this to the classroom, I made ten transparencies similar to the ones which follow. The category I selected was "Television Programs." Using an opaque sheet on top of the transparency, I revealed one line of consonants every five seconds.

The class was divided into two teams. The teams alternated turns but, during a team's turn, anyone on the team could call out guesses. Armed with my stopwatch to accurately reveal additional lines every five seconds, I could stop the clock the moment I heard the correct answer. The number of seconds was the team's score for that round. The team with the lowest score won.

My ten transparencies were quickly exhausted, but I had a stack of blanks and special transparency pencils available for all the students who begged to make their own *Baffle* sheets. Three student-created sequences follow.

Baffle: Student-made transparencies
(An opaque sheet of paper is placed on the transparency. The emcee reveals an additional line each five seconds until a member of the competing team calls out the correct answers. The category was "television programs.")

HLY
HLLY
HLLYW
HLLYWD
HLLYWDS
HLLYWDSQ
HLLYWDSQR
HLLYWDSQRS
HOLLYWDSQRS
HOLLYWODSQRS
HOLLYWOODSQRS
HOLLYWOODSQURS
HOLLYWOODSQUARS
HOLLYWOODSQUARES

SSM
SSMS
SSMST
SESMST
SESMSTR
SESMSTRT
SESAMSTRT
SESAMSTRET
SESAMESTRET
SESAMESTREET

TH
THPR
THPRT
THPRTR
THPRTRD
THPRTRDG
THPRTRDGF
THPRTRDGFM
THPRTRDGFML
THPRTRDGFMLY
THPARTRDGFMLY
THPARTRIDGFMLY
THPARTRIDGEFMLY
THPARTRIDGEFAMLY
THPARTRIDGEFAMILY
THEPARTRIDGEFAMILY

ALL
(A knowing laugh.)

THURSDAY #15 (accompanied by Tuesday and Wednesday)

Skills:

- vocabulary development
- determining meaning in context
- listening
- comprehension of tone and intent

This Thursday activity required some real advance work. Based on a description in the *Teacher's Guide to Television*, The Many Faces of Humor seemed a good show to videotape for future use. My idea was to use a comedy hour as the framework in which to introduce vocabulary words to my students. One of the real handicaps of a limited vocabulary is the inability to understand verbal jokes. I happen to feel very strongly about developing a sense of humor in my downtrodden kids.

While our videotape equipment was taping the show at school one night, I watched it at home, noting the vocabulary words that were crucial to understanding puns, jokes, and comedy situations. One portion of the show was an adult version of *Sesame Street* called *Caraway Street*. It was terrific for my purposes: there were plenty of innocuous references to sex (to interest the students) plus flashing words and symbols between skits.

On the Tuesday before the Thursday my classes were scheduled to watch the program, I gave them a list of 15 words to define in a very traditional fashion. The next day I divided the classes into small groups, assigning each group to write a very short story in which they used all 15 words. They did a terrific job and had time to share the stories at the end of the period.

The next day the reading classes convened in the videotape room to watch a comedy show. The next time I do this, I think I'll print up a "Rationale for Doing This" to distribute to bewildered observers.

Nevertheless, I really felt that the kids enjoyed the activity and gained a personal recognition of the difference WORDS can make in the way we experience all that is about us.

After the show, I asked which of the words they had been working with in class they had heard, and the context in which the words were used. In each class, students were able to answer my question completely and accurately.

STEVE

Hey, Miss McKee,
is he kin to you?
Is he, is he?

If he was at your
sister's high school,
ya think he'd bust her?

PETER C.

Contradictory statements, huh?

Okay. It says here there are
1,400 kids in the school.
Twenty were busted, right?
The principal said the
problem is

99 percent

solved.
The narc said 9 out of 10 kids
smoke. There's the contradiction.

And what's this about
pretending to smoke
but just not *inhaling*!
Ba-lone-y. I must say
BA-LONE-Y!

THURSDAY #16, et cetera

Skills:

all those previously mentioned
and more

Thursday #16, et cetera, I refer to as Read-and-Respond-To's. I initiated this activity by finding and making copies of high interest reading selections in newspapers, magazines, or wherever. After distributing the selections, an open discussion of the content followed. The interest level of the reading selections had to be high or the activity would have become tiresome. Following are selections that I consider appropriate; the first because the "narc" is indeed my first cousin, and the second because the whole school was involved in the community's reaction to the sex survey and the school's sex education program (or lack thereof).

Occasionally students brought me some Read-and-Respond-To's, and I would then make multiple copies to be used in the contributing student's class.

Undercover 'Narc' Nabs Students

By ROBERT W. FOWLER
Inquirer Staff Writer

West Chester police, employing an undercover narcotics agent who enrolled at Henderson Senior High School, arrested more than 20 students and dropouts Tuesday and charged them with selling or using marijuana, hashish, and cocaine.

Mayor J. Herbert Chambers commended the four-month investigation by undercover agent Dwight McKee, a long-haired, boyish-looking, 20, but said he was saddened that one of those arrested was his 18-year old granddaughter Elizabeth Chambers.

"I knew some of her friends were under investigation," Chambers said of his granddaughter, "I could have told her, but I wanted no special treatment for her. It comes a little bit close to home but you either do a job right or you don't do it at all."

Miss Chambers lives with her mother in Ridley Park and was not a student at the high school. She is charged with using marijuana.

McKee attended a community college in Harrisburg for two years before joining the West Chester Police Department last April. He attended police schools and worked with the Philadelphia narcotics unit for seven weeks before enrolling at Henderson under an assumed name last October.

"They didn't trust me at first because I was a new student," McKee said, "I didn't make my first buy until Nov. 28."

Ten of those arrested were charged with selling narcotics, the rest with using them. Eleven students were arrested at the school, and most of the others were arrested at their homes. Five were girls.

Mahwah Study Branded 'Filth'

By Jan Rubin

MAHWAH–The solicitation of student opinion on topics they feel should be included in the proposed health curriculum appears to have caused the objections of those parents who oppose the survey, according to John Stahura, president of the Board of Education.

In addition to hearing charges that the student survey was "filth" and was "doing wrong to our children," school board trustees Monday night heard some parents describe their minor children as their "wards" and demand the right of prior approval of materials made available to their offspring.

The student survey, promulgated and distributed by the Student Council Curriculum Committee, was designed to elicit student opinion on the family living-sex education portion of the health-education curriculum. The results will be offered to the citizens advisory committee, which is investigating a health curriculum for grades 3-12.

Working with their adviser, Carol Slusser, chairman of the curriculum committee, Dan Collishaw, Monica Ullrich and Gary Calleo developed the questionnaire, which was approved by the board and administration after a revision following its initial rejection by the superintendent.

The survey was distributed to high school students by their homeroom teachers and students had the option of filling out the survey and turning it back to the teacher unsigned or declining to respond and returning it.

The survey elicited opinions on whether family living and sex education should be included in the health program; whether sex education should be left entirely to parents, church, school or friends; the adequacy of the present program; the desirability of co-ed health classes; the inclusion of a variety of topics such as family planning, birth control, venereal diseases, child care, rape, pre-marital sex and male-female relationships; where the individual learned most about sex and from whom he or she received an adequate sex education.

Stahura said the list of topics surveyed appeared to have disturbed a few parents. Most of the parents, who discussed the survey at a recent Home-School Organization meeting, did not concur with the opposing parents, he added.

The same parents also tended to feel questions about where and from whom students received sex information are an invasion of the privacy of their home, Stahura said.

Mahwah Defense

At Monday's Board of Education meeting in Mahwah, some parents condemned as "filthy" and "disgusting" a survey of high school students' opinions on the family living-sex education portions of the health education program. Some felt parents should have been accorded the right of prior approval of the survey. Promulgated by the Student Council Curriculum Committee and circulated with the approval of board and administration, the survey results will be offered to the citizens advisory committee, which is looking into a health-education program for grades 3-12, for its edification.

We agree with the defense of the quality of the survey and the rights of high school students to make decisions within their realm of operations offered by Richard Gallivan, superintendent, and John Stahura, president of the Board of Education, and we commend both for their forthrightness. We congratulate Carol Slusser, chairman of the Student Council committee, and her colleagues Dan Collishaw, Monica Ullrich and Gary Calleo for a well-thought-out survey that will doubtless provide the advisory committee with valuable insights.

THERESA

Our whole class will do
"The Blue Hotel."

Ellen and I can do
sound effects
and take the two
female roles.

Now, if we're going to
practice,
let's not waste any more
time.

Everybody sit around here
on the rug.

Montgomery, that includes
you, too.

Remember, it's going to be
on tape,
so turn the pages
silently
and don't
giggle,
gentlemen.

THURSDAY #17, the week of

Skills:

silent reading for meaning
oral interpretation
understanding of character, plot sequence, and dramatic form

Students selected plays of their choice from the list which follows. Selection of a play was dependent on interest in the story and number of characters in the play.

On the first day, students selected groups and plays. Each student read the selected play in its entirety before character roles were chosen. On the second day, character roles were determined, and the play was rehearsed by reading the parts aloud. The third day was for additional rehearsal, including sound effects. On day four, the Reader's Theatre was tape recorded. The students knew that I intended to keep the recordings for future use with students who could read the plays and simultaneously listen to dramatic readings on earphones. On day five, or Game Day Friday, many students took the option of listening to their own Reader's Theatre taping or that of other groups or classes.

Title and Characters	Synopsis
The Glorious Whitewasher Announcer Tom Sawyer Aunt Polly Jim Ben Rogers Billy Fisher	Aunt Polly has ordered Tom to whitewash the fence in front of their house, but Tom would rather meet his friends or go swimming. A little thinking, a bit of scheming, and some psychology, and Tom turns his unpleasant chore into a profit-making enterprise.
The Night the Bed Fell James Briggs Father Mother Herman (Sound Effects)	While Briggs is visiting his cousin James, he quickly discovers that everything is not quite normal in his cousin's house. Briggs himself is not exactly "normal." This story is typical of the humor of its author, James Thurber.
The Necklace Announcer Monsieur Loisel Madame Matilde Loisel Madame Jeanne Forestier	A woman is invited to a very special party. Because she wants to look her very best, she borrows a necklace from a good friend. She loses the necklace and works long and hard to replace it. The author gives a special twist to the end of this play.

Title and Characters	Synopsis
A Service of Love Announcer Joe Larrabee Delia	Joe Larrabee and Delia Caruthers had both come to New York to make their fortunes. Joe was an artist. Delia was a singer. They met, fell in love, got married, and were very happy for a while. Their only trouble was their lack of money. Delia and Joe each had an idea, but they kept these ideas from each other. O' Henry's surprise ending showed them how close their ideas really were.
The Return of the Moresbys Announcer Richard Moresby Dr. Sing Editor Una Moresby Prouty Butler Sergeant	Mr. Moresby's wife believes that humans are reincarnated as animals. Her husband kills her before she can write a will. Una's dying promise is that she will avenge her own murder. Immediately after her death, Richard begins being troubled by various animals. He ultimately dies as a result of an accident caused by a cat, which he believes is the reincarnation of his wife.
Times Change Johnny Sanchez Barbara Sanchez Mrs. Sanchez Mr. Sanchez	Johnny Sanchez is president of a Mexican-American club at his high school. When the club decides to hold its meetings in Spanish, Johnny gets angry at his parents, believing that they thought so little of their heritage to bring him up speaking English. His father explains how he was handicapped by his difficulty with English, and Johnny understands that changing times mean changing priorities. His father then helps him learn Spanish.
The Blue Hotel Patrick Scully Johnny Scully Martha Scully Helen Scully Mr. Blanc Bartender Ullman Beaton Fraser Masters	Some men are playing cards in a hotel in Nebraska in the 1890s. They are joined by a traveller named Ullman, who believes someone is out to kill him. Ullman becomes involved in two fights and is killed in the second. One of the card players suggests that they were responsible for his death because they encouraged the fight.

KEVIN

I found the cartoon,
but what's a caricature and
a hyper-bowl?

"That's where they play
the New Year's Day
football game, dummy!"

(She's bringing me a
dictionary
and she told
fatmouth
to "refer to me
as Kevin.")

LOUIS

If I have to keep saying
"Who is Brendan T. Byrne?"
every time you say
"Governor of New Jersey,"
Then I wanna be called
Louis A. Rizzo, Jr.
all the time.

"Okay, Louis A. Rizzo all the time,
what does the A stand for?"

All the time!

(How do you like that one, gang?
And *he* thought he was so smart!)

THURSDAY #18, the newspaper unit

Skills:

- vocabulary development
- awareness of current events
- identification of lead paragraphs
- interpreting editorial cartoons
- finding the main idea of an editorial
- translating classified advertising abbreviations into complete words (spelling)
- making inferences
- drawing conclusions
- sequencing events

I had ordered classroom copies of the *Bergen Record* for a two-week period. The day before the newspapers began, I took all my freshmen to the publishing house. They were given a tour of the entire building, from the news desks to the press room. The next day they reported their observations to the other members of their classes. They were most fascinated by the teletype machines, the photography lab, and the press room.

For the next ten days, each student was to read the newspaper for at least fifteen minutes. The only required readings during this time were the lead paragraphs of all front page articles. I explained that the purpose of this was preparation for participation in the *Jeopardy Game* on the last day of the unit. The *Jeopardy Game* is described later, but the students would be quizzed daily on front page news in this manner: I would give a short answer, and a student would ask the correct question. This oral quiz occurred at the end of the period each day.

In addition to reading the newspaper, students were to complete three newspaper activity cards. I typed these activities on 5 x 9 inch cards cut from heavy oaktag, and covered each with transparent contact paper to make it permanent and washable.

HOROSCOPE DISCUSS or WRITE ON . . .

Some people believe that the position of the "stars" at the time of birth has a daily and lifelong effect. These people believe in *astrology*, the study of the stars.

In a horoscope, predictions are made according to one's astrological sign.

Here is an example:

> Pisces (Feb. 20–Mar. 20). Petty details are a nuisance to you. You are bored.

Discuss or write about your horoscope today.

INDIVIDUAL or SMALL GROUP

COMIC STRIPS DRAMATIZE

Cartoonists use humor as a form of expression. The words which appear in *dialogue balloons* could be understood differently, depending on the reader's tone.

Every detail in the drawings must be observed to understand the cartoonist's intent.

Dramatize at least two comic strips. You may memorize the actual dialogue from the balloons, but don't be afraid to improvise.

SMALL GROUP

Sample Newspaper Activity Cards (actual size: 5″ x 9″)

The Jeopardy Game

The *Jeopardy Game* is another classroom adaptation of a television program. As a part of the newspaper unit, its primary purpose is to review current events. However, I also use it for general purposes such as reviewing basic knowledge (state capitals, general math, etc.).

The class is divided into two teams. Student desks are arranged in rows. On the *Jeopardy* board are seven categories. The contestant selects a category and point value of the answer he wishes to hear. Prepared answers and questions can be written on index cards, which the emcee holds. The emcee provides the contestant with the answer of his choice, and the contestant must *ask the question* which would be correctly answered by the emcee's words. If the contestant asks the appropriate question—it must be in question form—he scores the point value. If he responds incorrectly, the point value is subtracted from his team's score. The question is then offered to any volunteer from the opposing team.

If the volunteer answers the question correctly (that is, asks the correct question), he earns the point value. If he is incorrect, however, he loses no points and it is still his team's turn.

Order of turns is determined by seating arrangement from the front of row 1 to the back of row 1, from the front of row 2 to the back of row 2, and so on. No one is allowed to answer out of turn.

Soon after the newspaper *Jeopardy Game*, one of my classes completely organized their own game. One student wrote all the answers and questions and acted as emcee. The rest of the class participated as contestants on two teams. The whole affair was videotaped and later enjoyed by all classes—as if they were watching a real television program.

The videotape is available to all teachers as a resource for organizing reviews in their own content areas. It would be especially effective, and purposeful, before an exam.

THE JEOPARDY BOARD
(drawn on the blackboard)*

LOCAL NEWS	NATIONAL NEWS	SYNONYMS	NEWS DEPT.	SPORTS
5	5	5	5	5
10	10	10	10	10
15	15	15	15	15
20	20	20	20	20
25	25	25	25	25

*As a category and point value are selected, the emcee erases the numerals.

Sample answers (given by emcee)	*Acceptable questions* (given by contestant)
Hank Aaron	Who beat Babe Ruth's homerun record?
3½ months ago	When was Patricia Hearst kidnapped?
Mahwah High School, June 2	Where will the Arts Festival be held?

VICKI

I wish my mother were alive.
I wish my father and I would get along.
I wish I had a lot of friends.
I wish I had all blue and yellow clothes.
I wish my dog would have puppies.
I wish I could get a maid.
I wish I had some help.

BONNIE

I love the smell of Robert Yager's
T-shirt.
It smells like some kind of soap.
It is soft and cuddly just like him.
If I could have any kind of clothing,
it would have to be Robert's T-shirt.
That's what I love the best.

PETER C.

The soft sand like a kitten's coat
crumbled below my feet.
The sun pounded down behind my back.
The water tingled between my toes.
Then it rained.
I was cold.

ELIZABETH

I hate the sound of
WHY?
It makes me crazy
CRAZY
And I could just
SCREAM!

THURSDAY #19, the *Poet Within* unit

Skills:

reading
writing
thinking
feeling
sharing

The *Poet Within* unit consists of nine writing exercises adapted from Kenneth Koche's *Wishes, Lies, and Dreams* for use with secondary school students. With some variations, I have used these techniques with seventh graders, with ninth graders, and now with ninth through twelfth grade remedial readers (predominantly male). I have *never* been disappointed when kids let that poet within out.

The assignments are introduced separately and verbally. The assignment sheet is distributed for reference only as the students compile their poetry collections.

All writing is done in a workshop atmosphere. I read many poems by well-known poets to illustrate the focus of each assignment, as well as some poems I have written myself. During the writing sessions, I look over shoulders whenever possible, and read aloud as many student poems as I can, as fast as they are written (with permission, of course). I offer suggestions for intensifying images. For reluctant writers, I offer the suggestions: "Think of your earliest childhood memories." or "Just write a paragraph and we'll turn it into a poem together." However, most students have no difficulty communicating in this medium. Of all high school students, I would venture to guess that my "losers" are less conforming and more capable of unique perceptions than their more academically able peers.

Each student had to compile a neat collection of his poems.

THE POET WITHIN

The result of your experimentation with self-expression, poetic techniques, and poetic sensitivity will be a collection of your own poetry.

Your poetry collections should include at least one example of each of the following writing exercises:

#1 I wish . . . (at least four lines beginning with these words)	Focus: repetition and real feelings
#2 Noise Poem (describe, or make your poem sound like, a wonderful or horrible sound)	Focus: auditory impressions
#3 Color Poem (write your associations with a color, or describe a vivid scene in which a color or colors dominate)	Focus: visual impressions
#4 Smell Poem (describe an aroma, an odor, a fragrance, or a smell with all its associations)	Focus: olfactory impressions
#5 Touch Poem (how does something feel? how does it make *you* feel?)	Focus: tactile impressions
#6 I am . . . (an animal or an inanimate object; use as many of the above focuses as possible)	Focus: personification
#7 Dream Poem	Focus: the subconscious
#8 I used to be . . . But now I am . . . (at least three couplets)	Focus: sequence, contrast
#9 I seem to be . . . But I really am . . . (at least three couplets)	Focus: awareness of roles and self

You may also include any additional poems.

STEVE

That's the best book I ever read!
Yeah, I got them to talk about it.
Then they asked me about baseball.
I was cool, okay.

They asked Bob to come back and
have lunch with them.

One kid asked me for my autograph.

THURSDAY #20, super sport reading program

This was an interschool reading program which I designed to meet the needs of my poorest readers. They needed self-confidence, a sense of enjoyment associated with reading, and recognition in areas other than sports.

Their outstanding abilities in sports, however, contributed to the success of the program. The fourth and fifth graders to whom my super sports read stories were themselves reluctant readers, and the program served the dual purpose of motivating both levels toward attitudinal changes.

I prepared all the super sports to read to small groups. As they practiced and practiced reading the picture books in the Reading Resource Room, the other students often gathered around to hear the stories. It was incredible. Each boy visited an elementary classroom four times. The first three times they read picture books and discussed the books with the students, as well as answered questions about the athletic achievements. On the fourth visit, the super sports read from their Poet Within collections. Then they supplied construction paper and felt markers for the younger kids to try their hands at an "I wish . . ." poem and an "I used to be/But now I am . . ." poem. The youngsters then returned to their classes with original poems.

I must credit the success of the super sport program to the support it received from my supervisor, the school principals, the classroom teachers, and the publicity given to it by the Board of Education newsletter. The news release which follows was compiled by me but was written by the super sports who wrote their own self-descriptions. This news release was distributed to all classroom teachers at the elementary school, so that the youngsters could anticipate the "big athletes" who were coming to, of all things, read to them.

Super Sport Reading Program – 1974

an interschool program for sharing the enjoyment of reading

Mahwah High School – Joyce Kilmer

It can be fun to share stories and talk about the experiences of the characters in books. If you don't believe that, just ask the high school athletes involved in the Super Sport Reading Program!

These athletes have already distinguished themselves in varsity sports like football, basketball, hockey, and baseball. Now they have become really "Super," because they will be visiting the Joyce Kilmer School to read stories, and talk about them, with small groups of students.

The Super Sports will share stories about the world's largest red dog, about a man who is too big to fit his bed or bathtub, about a turtle who wishes only to run faster, and about Leo, the Late Bloomer.

The Spring 1974 Super Sports are:

JACK FOX

Jack Fox, senior, has played football, basketball, and baseball for Mahwah High School. On the football field, he has been the punter, halfback, and defensive end.

Jack is currently a valuable player on the baseball team. He plans to continue playing baseball in the future.

CHRIS GIRO

Chris Giro, senior, played on the Mahwah football teams during his freshman, sophomore, and junior years.

In seventh and eighth grade, Chris became interested in wrestling as a manager. He continued this interest and has received many awards for wrestling.

He placed second in the Christmas tournament, second in the Districts, and received All League Honorable Mention.

STEVE PORTER

Senior Steve Porter plays football, basketball, and baseball. In football he received many honors: All League, All Bergen, All Suburban, All Area Honorable Mention, and All County Honorable Mention. He also won the Hatchet Award and was named Most Valuable Player.

Steve was selected to the Prep All American Team.

In baseball this season, Steve hit three homeruns in one game for a county record.

He plans to attend William Penn College in Iowa or to join the Rookie League in Florida. He has been scouted by the Pittsburgh Pirates, New York Mets, Boston Redsox, and Kansas City Royals.

ED SINCLAIR

Ed Sinclair is a junior. He was an outstanding member of the Mahwah High School varsity hockey team. He played on the starting line as defense man.

STEVE SOCHULAK

Steve Sochulak, senior, is a member of the varsity baseball team. He starts at first base for the Mahwah T-Birds. He has also played four years of football and basketball.

SCOT VAN DEMARK

Scot Van Demark was named to the All League and All Suburban football team as a junior.

He has participated in three years of varsity football, basketball, and track.

In the discus throw event, Scot has been ranked among the top ten in the state of New Jersey.

BOB VAN GROL

Bob Van Grol is a junior. He has played junior varsity and varsity football, sustaining injuries this year which unfortunately benched him for most of the season.

JOHN WEAVER

John Weaver is a junior. He participates in the high jump event on the Mahwah High School track team. He also played football and likes to ski.

All of the outstanding Super Sports are enrolled in Developmental Reading at the high school. Preparation for participation in the Super Sport Reading Program is one of their class activities. In addition, they are involved in a range of activities to improve reading and study skills.

Super Sport Reading Program – 1975

an interschool program for sharing the enjoyment of reading

Mahwah High School – Joyce Kilmer

It can be fun to share stories and talk about the experiences of the characters in books. If you don't believe that, just ask the high school athletes involved in the Super Sport Reading Program.

These athletes have distinguished themselves in varsity sports like football, wrestling, track, and basketball. Now they have become really "Super," because they will be visiting the Joyce Kilmer School to read stories, and talk about them, with the intermediate school students.

The Super Sports will read stories about a high school track star who realizes that the thrill and excitement of winning a race can never be the same the second time around ("Only Once Can a Race Be Won") and about a high school baseball team that proves itself better than the coach expects ("Two for the Book").

The Spring 1975 Super Sports are:

TODD BECKER

Todd Becker, junior, is a member of the varsity wrestling team at 108 lbs. He won the District Tournament and the Novice Tournament as a freshman at 98 lbs. This year he was named First Team All Suburban.

Todd has been a member of the wrestling and cross-country teams for two years.

MIKE CUMMINGS

Mike Cummings, junior, has been involved in three years of football as a guard and defensive tackle. He also is involved in varsity track for Mahwah High School. Mike runs the half-mile and the one mile.

TOM KORT

Tom Kort, sophomore, throws the shotput and discus on the Mahwah High School track team. He also plays linebacker and guard on the football team.

BOB VAN GROL

Bob Van Grol is a senior. He plays quarterback on the varsity football team. He is also a defensive halfback.

This is the second year Bob has participated in the Super Sport Reading Program.

MIKE WRIGHT

Mike Wright is a sophomore. He played halfback and linebacker on the freshman football team. He also played forward on the freshman basketball team.

This year Mike started on the junior varsity basketball team at guard position.

All the outstanding Super Sports are enrolled in reading courses at the high school. Preparation for participation in the Super Sport Reading Program is one of their class activities. In addition, they are involved in a range of activities to improve reading and study skills.

Super Sport Reading Program – 1976

an interschool program for sharing the enjoyment of reading

Mahwah High School – Joyce Kilmer

It can be fun to share stories and talk about the experiences of characters in books. If you don't believe that, just ask the high school athletes in the Super Sport Reading Program.

These athletes have distinguished themselves in several sports. In addition, they were enrolled in a course for Reading Improvement at the high school.

This year the Super Sport Program welcomes its first female athlete. Both Super Sports gained their "Super" reputations by participating in this interschool program, visiting the Joyce Kilmer School to read stories, and talk about them, with the intermediate school students.

The 1976 Super Sports will read stories about their favorite sports—hockey and baseball. The stories are about extraordinary people and events in the history of American sports. The titles give a few hints about the stories, and raise a few questions: "The Most Injured Man in Hockey," "The Odyssey of the Stanley Cup," "The One-Armed Big Leaguer," and "The Tag-Along."

This year's Super Sports are:

LISA COBB

Lisa is a junior. Since her freshman year, she has played starting positions on the varsity volleyball, basketball, and softball teams.

This year she was named First Team All League and Most Valuable Player on the volleyball team. The team was undefeated.

Lisa was also captain of the basketball team, starting as a forward. In some games, she also played center and guard. In her freshman year, she was named Most Improved Player and awarded Honorable Mention in the league.

As a sophomore, Lisa was captain of the softball team and started as a pitcher. She started this year as a catcher and also played the positions of pitcher and first baseperson.

MICHAEL MECH

Mike is a junior who has been playing on the high school hockey team for three years. He played defense, left wing, and goalie on the team that came in second in the state. Last year he was picked for an All Star team which traveled through the United States and Canada.

Mike has been skating for six years and has also played on other organized hockey teams.

He played defense and left wing on the high school soccer team, but hockey is his favorite sport.

SUMMERTIME

Summertime . . . and the living will not necessarily be easy for my students. Some will have jobs; some will enter colleges. Some will anticipate, with mixed emotions, the opening of school in September. Have I improved their reading ability?

Yes, there are marked improvements on the posttest of the Gates-MacGinitie. But now I must analyze the results. Was it the individually prescribed instruction faithfully completed during reading lab sessions? Was it the emphasis on externalization of thinking processes and refinement of thinking skills?

Of course, there was no scientific attempt to control variables. Variables like personality, modes of learning, physiological states—these all surely affect what happens in our classrooms. And then there is the variable of the reading process, that mysterious function of language that so enriches lives in the pragmatic realm of the real world and in the fantasy world of dreams and vicarious experiences.

Time for Reflection

I only know my students would have rebelled entirely against the structured, programed learning had there been no opportunity to vent their personalities, to achieve through their oral facility rather than tediously grappling with the printed page.

It was, as in all things, a balance that met their needs and my needs, that made the lab come alive with language, that made me eager to try again—next year.

References

Carlson, Thorsten. *Administrators and Reading.* New York: Harcourt Brace Jovanovich, 1972.

Daniels, Steven. *How 2 Gerbils . . . and I Taught Them How to Read.* Philadelphia: Westminster Press, 1971.

Della-Piana, Gabriel M. *Reading Diagnosis and Prescription: An Introduction.* New York: Holt, Rhinehart and Winston, 1968.

Fader, Daniel N., and Elton B. McNeil. *Hooked on Books: Program Proof.* New York: Berkley Publishing, 1968.

Farr, Roger. *Reading: What Can Be Measured?* Newark, Delaware: International Reading Association, 1969.

Goodman, Kenneth, and James Fleming (Eds.) *Psycholinguists and the Teaching of Reading.* Newark, Delaware: International Reading Association, 1969.

Gorman, Alfred. *Teachers and Learners: The Interactive Process of Education.* Boston: Allyn and Bacon, 1969.

Harris, Larry A., and Carl B. Smith. *Reading Instruction through Diagnostic Teaching.* New York: Holt, Rhinehart and Winston, 1972.

Harris, Larry A., and Carl B. Smith (Eds.). *Individualizing Reading Instruction.* New York: Holt, Rhinehart and Winston, 1972.

McKee, Donna R. "To the Student: A Learning Design for Developmental Reading," unpublished curriculum guide, New York University, 1973.

Moffett, James. *A Student Centered Language Arts Curriculum: Grades K–13.* New York: Houghton Mifflin, 1968.

Moyle, Donald. "The Reading Curriculum," lecture at Montclair, New Jersey, State College, April 22, 1974.

Pendrak, Michael. "Performance Contracting and the Secondary School Reading Lab," *Journal of Reading,* 17 (March 1974).

Sobel, Donald J. *Two-Minute Mysteries.* New York: Scholastic Book Services, 1967.

Stanford, Gene, and Barbara Dodds Stanford. *Learning Discussion Skills through Games.* New York: Citation Press, 1969.

Thomas, Ellen Lamar, and H. Alan Robinson. *Improving Reading in Every Class: A Sourcebook for Teachers.* Boston: Allyn and Bacon, 1973.